Modern Gikuyu

A concise introduction to the Kikuyu language

Modern Gikuyu
A concise introduction to the Kikuyu language

kasahorow Editors

Modern Gikuyu: a concise introduction to the Kikuyu language

by kasahorow Editors

Series: kasahorow Language Guides

ISBN 978-1494201999
1st Printing
©kasahorow.org. Read Gikuyu. Every day.

Contents

Index

List of Tables

Preface

All mistakes are ours.

License

You may freely photocopy and redistribute this book for private or commercial use. No restrictions. Yes you do not need our permission. Do good.

Errata

Write to us at
  gikuyu@kasahorow.org.

Chapter 1

Modern Gikuyu

Modern Gikuyu is a more readable form of written Gikuyu.

This short guide is designed to get you up to speed quickly with the modern Gikuyu language. We hope that after getting through it you will be able to read, write and speak basic Gikuyu sentences to express the following range of concepts:

1. I love you
2. Omari and Abdi are boys
3. John came here before I did
4. Who is that?
5. Amina will come home tomorrow
6. I came, I saw, I conquered

7. They do not like that
8. How did they eat five pizzas in two hours?
9. The family has entered their new house
10. Stop eating and hurry up!

For teachers of Gikuyu, this guide should provide you a basic outline for getting your new language learners to master the basic structure of the Gikuyu language. **Modern Gikuyu** is a spelling system for Gikuyu that uses spaces to separate pronouns from verbs. It is the spelling system used in this book.

1.1   Some explanations

In the text, any text marked with * indicates ungrammatical usage. Bolded text can be looked up in the index. The guide attempts to use plain English the first time a concept is explained; in this case the technical term is included in square brackets.

Pronunciations are surrounded by /.../ signs.

Written form   a
Spoken form   /a/

English translations are placed in italics in [ ] near their Gikuyu renditions.

We hope that this guide will help open up the culture of the Gikuyu-speaking peoples all over the world to you.

Chapter 2

Reading Gikuyu

The easiest way to learn the rules [**grammar**] of a language is to read text written in that language. This section will help you analyse Gikuyu texts to extract meaning from them.

2.1 Recognising letters

Gikuyu is written with 20 letters [**alphabet**] (2.1).

Aa	Bb	Cc	Dd	Ee	Gg
Hh	Ii	Ĩĩ	Jj	Kk	Mm
Nn	Oo	Rr	Tt	Uu	Ũũ
Ww	Yy				

Table 2.1: Gikuyu alphabet

2.2 Recognising words

The main types of words--**parts of speech**--used in Gikuyu are those that represent persons, places, things or ideas--**nouns**, and actions--**verbs**.

2.2.1 Nouns

The nouns in every language are unlimited. Everything that has a name is a noun. Nouns can be represented by a single word or a group of words. Languages grow by making up new nouns to represent new things.

There are two main types of Modern Gikuyu nouns:

> **person nouns**, and

> **regular nouns**.

Note that formal written Gikuyu often has up to 10 types of nouns!

Gikuyu nouns dictate a lot about how the other parts of speech in a sentence are written down. This behaviour is called **concord** because all the parts of speech must agree with each other in a grammatically correct sentence.

When there is just one item of the noun [**singular**]

or the noun cannot be counted, you do not need to modify the spelling in any way. When there is more than one [**plural**] of the noun, the spelling is modified to indicate this.

Regular nouns and person nouns form their plurals differently.

Person nouns

Person nouns generally begin with **mũ** when referring to the singular person. When referring to the plural, **mũ** [/mo/] is replaced by **a** [/a/] at the beginning (**prefix**) of the person noun.

Where the singular begins with **ka**, it is replaced in the plural by **tũ**.

	Singular	Plural
Gikuyu	**mũ**tumia	**a**tumia
English	woman	women
Gikuyu	**mũ**thuri	**a**thuri
English	man	men
Gikuyu	**ka**irĩtu	**tũ**irĩtu
English	girl	girls
Gikuyu	**ka**hĩĩ	**tũ**hĩĩ
English	boy	boys

Table 2.2: Person nouns

Regular nouns

Regular nouns form plurals predictably depending on their meaning (**semantic class**).
So if the singular starts with **mũ**, the plural is formed by changing **mũ** to

- **a** if a person, or

- **mĩ** if not a person.

If the singular starts with **gĩ**, the plural is formed by changing **gĩ** to **i**.

When in doubt, try with **mũ** as the singular prefix, and **ma** as the plural prefix for nouns.

Suggests	Singular	Plural
not a person	**mũ**	**mĩ**
	mũtĩ [tree]	mĩtĩ [trees]
	mũrango [door]	mĩrango [doors]
	mũkebe [tin]	mĩkebe [tins]
objects	gĩ	i
	gĩtĩ [seat]	itĩ [seats]
	gĩkombe [cup]	ikombe [cups]
	gĩtanda [bed]	itanda [beds]
objects	rĩ	ma
	rĩitho [eye]	maitho [eyes]

Table 2.3: Regular nouns and their meaning-based groups.

2.2.2 Describe Nouns - Adjectives

The quality of a noun is described by **adjectives**. Adjectives are placed after the noun. For example,

nyũmba njerũ [<u>new</u> house].

Again, since the noun dictates the form of all the other parts of speech, there are also two main types of adjectives:

- **person adjectives**, and

- **regular adjectives**.

Each adjective used to describe a noun must agree with the noun.
Adjectives take the same prefixes as nouns.

11

Person adjectives

When an adjective describes a singular person noun, **mũ** is attached in front of the adjective. In older texts, this may also be represented as **mw**.

When referring to a plural person noun, **a** is attached to the front of the adjective. In older texts, the **a** may not be present since in the spoken form it is hardly distinct from the next vowel in the adjective.

	Singular	Plural
Swahili	m̲ũtumia **mũerũ**	a̲tumia **aerũ**
English	**new** wife	**new** wives
Swahili	m̲ũiritũ m̲ũthaka	a̲iritũ **athaka**
English	**beautiful** lady	**beautiful** ladies
Swahili	m̲ũrutani **mũũrũ**	a̲rutani **aũrũ**
English	**bad** teacher	**bad** teachers

Table 2.4: Adjectives **erũ**, **thaka**, and **ũrũ** with person nouns.

Regular adjectives

Regular adjectives form alliterations with the nouns they are describing.

As with nouns, when in doubt, try with **mũ** as the

mũ	mĩ
mũrango **mũerũ** [**new** door]	mĩrango **mĩerũ** [**new** doors]
mũti **mũega** [**good** tree]	mĩti **mĩega** [**good** trees]

gĩ	nj
gĩti **kĩerũ** [**new** chair]	iti **njerũ** [**new** chairs]
gĩti **kĩega** [**good** chair]	iti **njega** [**good** chairs]

rĩ	ma
ritho **rĩerũ** [**new** eye]	maitho **maerũ** [**new** eyes]
rĩtho **rĩega** [**good** eye]	maitho **maega** [**good** eyes]

mũ	ma
ũthiũ **mũerũ** [**new** face]	mothiũ **maerũ** [**new** faces]
ũthiũ **mũega** [**good** face	mothiũ **maega** [**good** faces]

Table 2.5: Adjectives **erũ** and **ega** with regular nouns.

singular prefix, and **ma** as the plural prefix for adjectives.

2.2.3 Determiners

Where there is an article, it is written after the noun.

- **definite articles**
  kairĩtu <u>kau</u> [<u>the</u> *girl*], **kahĩĩ** <u>kau</u> [<u>the</u> *boy*]
  kahĩĩ <u>karĩa</u> [<u>that</u> *boy*]

- **indefinite articles**
  kahĩĩ [<u>a</u> *boy*, or, *boy*]
  mũgima [<u>an</u> *adult*, or, *adult*]
  kahĩĩ o ũguo [<u>some</u> *boy*]

2.2.4   Pronouns

Happily, pronouns can stand in for any noun. Which means that if you don't know the name of something, point at it and use a pronoun to refer to it instead!

There are two main types--just like the nouns they refer to:

person pronouns, and

regular pronouns.

Person pronouns

Subject pronouns usually replace a person noun at the beginning of a sentence. All subject pronouns come before a verb. For example,

nĩ ria [*I eat*].

In older texts, the pronoun is usually written together with the verb as **nĩ**ria.

Object pronouns come right before the verb when used. Object pronouns, listed in Table 2.7, are also written alone. For example,

Nĩũ **nye** ndete [*(You **me** love*) You love **me***].

nĩ	*I*	ndi	*not I*
nĩũ	*you*	ndũ	*not you*
nĩa	*she/he*	nda	*not she/not he*
nĩtũ	*we*	tũti	*not we*
nĩmũ	*you (plural)*	mũti	*not you (plural)*
nĩma	*they*	mati	*not they*

Table 2.6: Subject pronouns for person nouns

nĩa **nye** ndete	he loves **me**
nĩa **kwe** ndete	he loves **you**
nĩa **mwe** ndete	he loves **her**
nĩa **mwe** ndete	she loves **him**
nĩa **twe** ndete	he loves **us**
nĩa **mwe** ndete	he loves **you (plural)**
nĩa **me** ndete	he loves **them**

Table 2.7: Object pronouns for person nouns.

Regular pronouns

Regular pronouns behave similarly. But there are only two to remember: **it**, and **they/them**.

They are placed right before the verb whenever they are used. Look at this example involving **gũ thoma** [*to read*]

Ibuku rĩrĩ. Nĩ-ndi-**rĩ**-thoma
[*This book. I have read **it***].

Mabuku maya. Nĩ-ndi-**ma**-thoma

16

*[These books. I have read **them**]*

Interrogative pronouns, listed in Table 2.8, are used to ask questions.

Gikuyu	English
nũ	who
nĩkĩ	what
nĩkĩ gĩtũmi	why
kũ	where
atĩa	how
ĩrĩkũ	which

Table 2.8: Interrogative pronouns.

2.2.5 Verbs

Remember to ask yourself whenever you see a Gikuyu verb:

- what is the indication of the period of time in which the action took place [**tense**]?,

The Infinitive - Describe the verb's action

In English, the infinitive is indicated by **to** placed before the verb. In Gikuyu, it is either **kũ**, or **gũ** if the verb starts with **c, k, t, th** or a vowel.

Gikuyu	English
gũ ika	to do
gũ kua	to die
gũ thoma	to read
kũ geithia	to greet
kũ ria	to eat

Table 2.9: Infinitive verbs

Present Habitual - Action takes place habitually

This is for actions that take place on a regular basis [**habitual tense**]. Note that this tense doesn't use special pronouns.

Gikuyu	Literal English
nĩĩ nĩ thoma**ga**	Me, I read **habitually**
Amina nĩa thoma**ga**	Amina, she reads **habitually**

Table 2.10: Simple present habitual tense.

Present Continuous - Action is taking place

This is for an action in the process of taking place. It is indicated with **ra** in front of the verb.

Gikuyu	Literal English
nĩ **ra**thoma	I **am** read**ing**
Amina nĩa **ra**thoma	Amina, she **is** read**ing**

Table 2.11: Simple present continuous tense.

Past - Action took place in the past

The simple past is indicated by adding **ra** to the front of the verb AND replacing the **a** at the end of the verb with **ire**.

Gikuyu	Literal English
nĩ **ra**thek**ire**	I cook**ed**
Amina nĩa **ra**thek**ire**	Amina, she cook**ed**

Table 2.12: Past simple tense.

Future - Action will take place

The future tense is indicated by inserting the Gikuyu for *will* in front of the verb. *will* is indicated by **ka** or **ga** if the verb starts with **c, k, t, th** or a vowel.

Gikuyu	Literal English
nĩ **ga**thoma	I **will** read
Amina nĩa **ga**thoma	Amina, she **will** read
nĩ **ka**ria	I **will** eat
Amina nĩa **ka**ria	Amina, she **will** eat

Table 2.13: Future simple tense.

2.2.6 Describe Verbs - Adverbs

Adverbs describe the intensity of an action.
Like **adjectives**, **adverbs** are also placed after the verb. For example,

> we nĩũ rĩaga **ihenya** [*you, you eat **quickly***].

2.3 Recognising sentences

There are three main sentence patterns you can use to communicate with others:

- making a statement [**declarative sentences**]

- asking a question [**interrogative sentences**]

- commanding [**imperative sentences**]

Making a statement

e.g. *I love you.*

Gikuyu Word Order	ni	kwe	ndete
Grammar	[Noun]	[Noun]	[Verb]
	required	*optional*	*required*
Literally*	I	you	love

So in the negative, *I do not love you* will follow the same pattern:

Gikuyu Word Order	ndi	kwe	ndete
Grammar	[Noun]	[Noun]	[Verb]
	required	*optional*	*required*
Literally*	not I	you	love

Asking a question

e.g. *Where are you going?*

Gikuyu Word Order	Wa	thĩĩ	kũ?
Grammar	[Noun]	[Verb]	[Interrogative pronoun]
	required	*required*	*required*
Literally*	You	go	where?

Commanding

e.g. *Stop making noise!*

Gikuyu Word Order	Tiga	kũnegena!
Grammar	[Verb]	[Noun]
	required	*optional*
Literally*	Stop	making noise!

2.3.1 Forming complex sentences

Conjunctions allow you to combine two or more similar components. These components may be two or more. For example, two nouns, or, three verbs, or five sentences.

Some common conjunctions are listed in Table 2.14.

Gikuyu	Omari **na** Abdi	rĩai **na mũcoke** mũkome
English	Omari **and** Abdi	eat **and then** sleep
Gikuyu	Omari **kana** Abdi	nĩakomete **kwoguo** koma
English	Omari **or** Abdi	I am sleeping **so** sleep
Gikuyu	**Akorwo** Amina ...	**Akorwo** Amina nĩagũka **nawe,** ...
English	**If** Amina ...	**If** Amina comes **then** ...
Gikuyu	**Ngĩ** ...	**Ona ndakorwo** ngomete ...
English	**While, When** I ...	**Even if** I sleep ...

Table 2.14: Common conjunctions.

Prepositions on the other hand are placed after nouns to indicate the position of some other noun. Table 2.15 lists some common prepositions.

23

Gikuyu	nĩ **ta** fufu	**ta ũrĩa** Buliva aroigire
English	it is **like** fufu	**as** Buliva said
Gikuyu	thĩĩ **ni**	thĩĩ **thĩ**
English	go **in**	go **down**
Gikuyu	thĩĩ **mbere ya** Amina oke	thĩĩ **ume** haha
English	go **before** Amina comes	go **from** here
Gikuyu	ũka **hakuhĩ** nanĩĩ	thĩĩ **thutha**
English	come **near** me	go **behind**

Table 2.15: Common prepositions.

The following sentence patterns therefore become easy to understand:

Omari a-rathĩĩ cukuru
[*Omari, he-go school
(Omari is going to school)]

Omari na Abdi ma-rathĩĩ cukuru
[*Omari and Abdi, they-go school
(Omari and Abdi are going to school)]

Omari na Abdi wa nĩma-komete mbere ya ma-thĩĩ cukuru
[*Omari and Abdi, they are sleeping before they go school
(Omari and Abdi are sleeping before they go to school)]

2.4 How to use a dictionary

Entries are listed first in order of appearance of their first letter. If the first letters are the same, they are further listed in order of appearance of their second letter. If the second letters are the same, they are further listed in order of appearance of their third letter. And so on.

Nouns are listed in the singular form. **kahĩĩ** [boy]

Verbs are listed in their positive form without the infinitive prefix. **thoma** [read]

Adjectives are listed without any indicator of noun agreement. **erũ** [new]

Chapter 3

Understanding Gikuyu

You now know enough Gikuyu to understand basic speech and written text. You also know enough Gikuyu to make yourself understood.

If you find yourself unable follow spoken Gikuyu, ask the speaker to slow down their rate of talking. At the slower speed, you should be able to pick up enough words to make sense of what is being said.

Aria kahora [Speak slowly]

Arm yourself with a dictionary, get a verb practice book, and take on some reading material.

With your new found knowledge, and a dictionary, you should be able to translate the following sentences from Gikuyu:

1. Ni kwe ndete
2. Omari na Abdi nĩ tũhĩĩ
3. Johana arakinyire haha mbere ya njũke
4. Nũ ũcio?
5. Amina agoka mũciĩ rũciũ
6. Ndokire, ngĩona, ngĩhotana
7. Matiendete ũguo
8. Marahotire atĩa kũrĩa pizza ithano na mathaa merĩ?
9. Andũ acio a mũciĩ ũcio nĩmaraingĩrire nyũmba yao njerũ
10. Tiga kũrĩa na ũhiũhe!

Chapter 4

Useful Phrases

Here are some handy phrases that you should memorize to fill in the silence while you frantically think of how to say something complicated.

Hello	Wĩ mwega?
How are you?	Ũhana atĩa?
I am fine	Ndĩ mwega
And you?	Ĩĩ we?
Goodbye	Tigwo na wega
Later	Mathaa mangĩ
Good morning	Ũhoro wa rũcinĩ?
Good afternoon	Ũhoro wa mĩaraho?
Good evening	Ũhoro wa hwaĩ-inĩ?
Good night	Ũtukũ mwega
Sleep well	Koma wega

What is your name?	Wĩtagwo atĩa?
My name is Janet	Rĩtwa rĩakwa nĩ Janeti
I come from France	Nyumĩte Baranja
I am a ...	Ndĩ mũ ...
I am a teacher	Ndĩ mũrutani

| I am hungry | Ndĩ mũhũtu |
| I am thirsty | Ndĩ mũnyotu |

I like ...	Nĩnyendete ...
I want ...	Ndĩrenda ...
I don't like ...	Ndiendete ...
I don't want ...	Ndikwenda ...

| It is a bit expensive | Nĩ kĩa goro hanini |
| It is not expensive | Ti kĩa goro |

Yes	Ĩĩ
No	Aca
Please	Ndagũthaitha
Sorry	Njohera
Thank you	Thengiũ

What is the time?	Nĩ thaa cigana?
The time is ...	Nĩ thaa ...
The time is 2 o'clock	Nĩ thaa inyanya ĩrũngiĩ

Congratulations!

Nĩwĩkĩte wega!

Index

http://kasahorow.org/gikuyu

0-7 years

My First Kikuyu Dictionary

8-12 years

102 Gikuyu Verbs
Gikuyu Children's Dictionary

12 years and older

Modern Gikuyu
Gikuyu Learner's Dictionary

Printed in Great Britain
by Amazon.co.uk, Ltd.,
Marston Gate.